COUNTRIES

INDIA

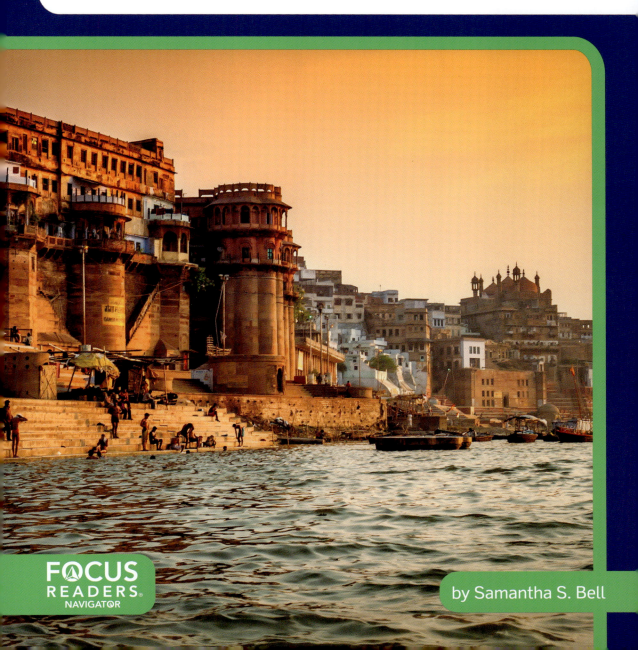

by Samantha S. Bell

WWW.FOCUSREADERS.COM

Copyright © 2025 by Focus Readers®, Mendota Heights, MN 55120. All rights reserved. No part of this book may be reproduced or utilized in any form or by any means without written permission from the publisher.

Focus Readers is distributed by North Star Editions:
sales@northstareditions.com | 888-417-0195

Produced for Focus Readers by Red Line Editorial.

Content Consultants: Afroz Taj, PhD, Associate Professor of Asian and Middle Eastern Studies, and John Caldwell, PhD, Teaching Associate Professor of Asian and Middle Eastern Studies, University of North Carolina at Chapel Hill

Photographs ©: Shutterstock Images, cover, 1, 4–5, 16, 19, 20–21, 25, 26–27; Red Line Editorial, 7; iStockphoto, 8–9, 11, 14–15, 28; Mario De Biasi/Mondadori Portfolio/Sipa USA/AP Images, 13; Shashi S. Kashyap/Hindustan Times/Getty Images, 23

Library of Congress Cataloging-in-Publication Data
Names: Bell, Samantha, author.
Title: India / by Samantha S. Bell.
Description: Mendota Heights, MN: Focus Readers, [2025] | Series:
  Countries | Includes bibliographical references and index. | Audience:
  Grades 4-6
Identifiers: LCCN 2024035804 (print) | LCCN 2024035805 (ebook) | ISBN
  9798889982241 (hardcover) | ISBN 9798889982807 (paperback) | ISBN
  9798889983866 (ebook pdf) | ISBN 9798889983361 (ebook other)
Subjects: LCSH: India--Juvenile literature.
Classification: LCC DS407 .B46 2025 (print) | LCC DS407 (ebook) | DDC
  954--dc23/eng/20240823
LC record available at https://lccn.loc.gov/2024035804
LC ebook record available at https://lccn.loc.gov/2024035805

Printed in the United States of America
Mankato, MN
012025

ABOUT THE AUTHOR
Samantha S. Bell lives in the foothills of the Blue Ridge Mountains with her family and lots of cats. She is the author of more than 150 nonfiction books for kids from kindergarten through high school. She loves learning about the different countries and cultures that are part of our amazing world.

TABLE OF CONTENTS

CHAPTER 1
Welcome to India 5

CHAPTER 2
History 9

CHAPTER 3
Climate, Plants, and Animals 15

CLIMATE CRISIS IN INDIA
Rain, Storms, and Heat 18

CHAPTER 4
Resources, Economy, and Government 21

CHAPTER 5
People and Culture 27

Focus Questions • 30
Glossary • 31
To Learn More • 32
Index • 32

CHAPTER 1

WELCOME TO INDIA

India is a large country in southern Asia. The Arabian Sea lies to the west. The Bay of Bengal is to the east. Seven other countries share borders with India.

The Himalayas are in the north of India. This mountain range contains the world's highest mountains. Melting ice from Himalayan **glaciers** flows down. The

> The city of Chennai is located on the Bay of Bengal in southeastern India.

5

water joins major river systems, including the Ganges River. The Ganges empties into the Bay of Bengal.

Southern India has mountain ranges, too. The Eastern and Western Ghats are there. A flatter area lies between them. This plateau is called the Deccan.

India is made up of 28 different states. The country also has eight **territories**. New Delhi is the capital of India. This city is located in northern India. Mumbai is another major city. Mumbai is on India's west coast.

India is home to more than 1.4 billion people. It has the largest population of any country in the world. The people of

India have many different languages, religions, and backgrounds. Together, they help create India's diverse culture.

MAP OF INDIA

CHAPTER 2

HISTORY

Humans have lived in India for thousands of years. Major rivers like the Indus and the Ganges provided water for India's earliest civilization. Between 5000 and 2000 BCE, people developed advanced writing and plumbing systems.

Over time, waves of people moved into and out of the area. Many came through

> The name *India* comes from the Indus River.

the Himalayas. Others came by sea. They crossed the Indian Ocean. Those movements led to a diverse population. Many kingdoms existed across the area. Societies and rulers changed and shifted over time, too.

Around 320 CE, the Gupta Empire was founded in northern India. It was led by the Gupta **dynasty**. This dynasty lasted about 200 years. Art and literature thrived during this period.

In 1206, the Delhi Sultanate was founded. It was the first Muslim kingdom in northern India. For hundreds of years, various dynasties ruled it. Then, in 1526, a ruler called Bābur came to power. He

Jama Masjid in Delhi was built during Mughal rule. The dynasty was one of India's richest and longest-ruling.

founded the Mughal Empire. This dynasty ruled from 1526 to 1857.

In the early 1600s, British traders came to India. They wanted to expand their East India Company. Over time, Britain **colonized** many areas. In 1857, Indian people fought back. They tried to rebel against British rule. The First War of Independence lasted until 1859. But the British kept control. India became part of the British Empire.

The British ruled India for the next 90 years. Their rule was known as the British Raj. During this time, the British fought in two world wars and other conflicts. They used India's resources and troops. The British had already **exploited** Indian people for centuries. The Raj made these problems worse.

Two years after the end of World War II (1939–1945), the people of India gained independence. In 1947, a British judge drew a new border. It separated India

Kolkata was India's biggest city until the 1980s.

and Pakistan. More Hindus lived in India. More Muslims lived in Pakistan.

Religious killings happened on both sides of the new border. So did riots. Many Muslims fled to Pakistan. And many Hindus and Sikhs fled to India. Millions of people died. Religious conflicts still play a role in India's politics today.

CHAPTER 3

CLIMATE, PLANTS, AND ANIMALS

Most of India has a warm climate. Temperatures are even hotter in desert areas. However, the country's northern regions can get very cold.

Monsoons are a key part of India's climate. Monsoon season usually lasts from June to September. Most of India's rain falls during this time. The

> The Thar Desert is located in northwestern India.

15

The Indian peacock is the country's national bird.

northeastern state of Meghalaya often receives the most rainfall. It is one of the wettest regions in the world.

India is home to many types of wildlife. Bengal tigers are famous. These tigers live in warm forests and wetlands. Monkeys called langurs live across some regions. Red pandas and Asian elephants are other iconic animals in India.

India's plants vary across habitats. Forests cover nearly a quarter of the country. Small shrubs grow in the desert. Neem trees are a common native plant. People use neem for medicines and skin products. Also, India produces more mangoes than any other country.

INDIA'S NATIONAL FLOWER

India's national flower is the lotus. It grows in shallow waters across the country. The flowers are pink or white. People cook and eat the seeds. They use some pieces for makeup and medicines. The lotus is also meaningful in other ways. In Indian culture, the lotus stands for purity and beauty. Lotus designs often appear in art. The Bahá'í temple south of New Delhi is shaped like a lotus bud.

CLIMATE CRISIS IN INDIA

RAIN, STORMS, AND HEAT

Climate change threatens India in several ways. Himalayan glaciers are a key source of water. But rising temperatures are affecting the glaciers. They are melting rapidly. People could lose that water source soon.

In some areas, higher heat is leading to less rain. That makes farming difficult. Crops do not get enough water. That means farmers make less money. People also do not get enough food. Other areas receive too much rain. For example, climate change makes monsoon season stronger and longer. Heavy rainfall leads to flooding. Landslides hurt people and destroy buildings.

Climate change affects other storms, too. It makes **cyclones** stronger. Cyclones form over the Indian Ocean. Then they move onto land.

Flooding in city streets can make it hard for people to get to work and school.

Often, cyclones damage farms and towns in India. They may also kill people.

Disease is another danger related to climate change. For example, mosquitoes spread malaria. A mosquito **parasite** carries the disease. The parasite grows faster in warmer weather. It spreads more quickly, too. In the early 2020s, India greatly reduced its number of malaria cases. But mosquitoes were finding new warm habitats. That made the problem more dangerous.

CHAPTER 4

RESOURCES, ECONOMY, AND GOVERNMENT

India's economy is huge. It includes many major industries. For example, the country has one of the world's biggest entertainment industries. India also produces more cars than most countries.

Technology is another major area of business. Many computer companies are based in western India. Foreign

Much of India's economy is cashless, including at markets. India records more digital transactions than any other country.

21

tech companies often hire Indian tech workers.

Many of India's big industries are based in Mumbai. Mumbai's location is great for shipping. The city has a huge port. That helps people trade with other countries. Mumbai is also a major banking center. The jewelry industry is based there, too.

MEGA MOVIES

India's movie industry is enormous. The country produces hundreds of films every year. Most films are made in three major cities. The largest production center is Hyderabad. Mumbai and Chennai also produce many films. Many films focus on love and romance. Indian films are often full of music. Their songs and dances are famous across the world.

Shah Rukh Khan is one of the most famous Indian actors.

India has many natural resources. Some resources include coal and diamonds. India is also one of the biggest producers of iron ore. People use this material to make steel.

Agriculture is another big part of India's economy. Millions of Indians have jobs related to farming. Major crops in India include rice, wheat, and cotton.

India also produces large amounts of milk, coffee, and spices. Some of these products are used in India. Many are exported to other countries.

Indian handicrafts are well known around the world. Some common handicrafts include clothing, carpets, and pottery. These items are often purchased abroad. Others are sold throughout India.

India's government is the largest democracy in the world. The president is the country's official leader. But India's prime minister has the most power. This person is the head of the government. India has a parliament, too. This group makes the country's laws. The parliament

In 2024, more than 640 million people voted in India's general election.

is made up of two parts. One is the Lok Sabha. That is the House of the People. The other part is the Rajya Sabha. That is the Council of States. States across India have their own governments, too. Each has a capital city and a chief minister.

CHAPTER 5

PEOPLE AND CULTURE

India is full of diverse people and cultures. People speak nearly 2,000 languages and **dialects** across the country. The government uses two official languages. They are Hindi and English.

Indians follow a variety of religions as well. About 80 percent of people are Hindu. About 14 percent are Muslim.

India's Smart Cities Mission began in 2015. It aims to increase technology in cities across the country.

The Golden Temple in Amritsar is an important holy site for Sikhs worldwide.

Other religions include Christianity, Sikhism, and Buddhism.

Traditional arranged marriages are common in India. In arranged marriages, families choose spouses for younger family members. They pick based on shared community and social status.

As in most societies, food is a big part of Indian culture. Meals are social events. Many Indians are vegetarians. Across India, meals often include spicy dishes. People eat them with rice or flatbreads. These customs all add to India's fascinating culture.

CELEBRATING WITH COLOR

Holidays are important in Indian culture. Many Indian people celebrate Holi. Holi is the Hindu festival of colors. The holiday happens every March. It marks the beginning of spring. During Holi, people throw colored powder. Holi often involves singing and dancing, too. Participants may also light bonfires to celebrate the holiday.

FOCUS QUESTIONS

Write your answers on a separate piece of paper.

1. Write a paragraph explaining the main ideas of Chapter 4.

2. If you visited India, what would you be most interested in seeing?

3. When did the Mughal Empire begin?
    - **A.** 1526
    - **B.** 1857
    - **C.** 1947

4. Why would farmers make less money during dry periods?
    - **A.** People don't want to buy crops during dry periods.
    - **B.** Crops don't grow as well, so farmers have less to sell.
    - **C.** Farms have too many crops, so prices go down.

Answer key on page 32.

GLOSSARY

climate change
A human-caused global crisis involving long-term changes in Earth's temperature and weather patterns.

colonized
Took control of an area by force and exploited its resources and population.

cyclones
Storms with strong rotating winds.

dialects
Forms of a language that are specific to groups of people.

dynasty
A series of rulers who all come from the same family.

exploited
Used unfairly.

glaciers
Large, slow-moving bodies of ice.

monsoons
Strong winds that bring periods of heavy rain to an area.

parasite
An organism that can grow in the body and cause sickness.

territories
Areas under government control that are not states.

TO LEARN MORE

BOOKS
Doeden, Matt. *Travel to India.* Minneapolis: Lerner Publications, 2022.
Phillips-Bartlett, Rebecca. *India.* Buffalo, NY: Gareth Stevens Publishing, 2024.
Van, R. L. *India.* Minneapolis: Abdo Publishing, 2023.

NOTE TO EDUCATORS
Visit **www.focusreaders.com** to find lesson plans, activities, links, and other resources related to this title.

INDEX

British Raj, 12

climate change, 18–19

economy, 21, 23

farming, 18–19, 23
food, 18, 29

Ganges River, 6–7, 9
glaciers, 5, 18

government, 12, 24–25, 27

Himalayas, 5, 7, 10

independence, 12
Indian Ocean, 7, 10, 18
Indus River, 7, 9

languages, 7, 27

monsoons, 15, 18
Mumbai, 6–7, 22

natural resources, 23
New Delhi, 6–7, 17

religions, 7, 13, 27–28

technology, 21–22

wildlife, 16

Answer Key: 1. Answers will vary; 2. Answers will vary; 3. A; 4. B